CHEERLEADING

Junior Sports

Morgan Hughes

Rourke
Publishing LLC
Vero Beach, Florida 32964

www.rourkepublishing.com

PHOTO CREDITS: p 5, 6, 9, 11, 12, 15, 18, 19, 22, 23, 26, 28, Pat Macbeth; p 13 Andy Lyons/Getty; p 16 Jonathan Daniel/Getty; p 20 Joel Nito/Getty; p 25 Ronald Martinez/Getty, title page, p 29 Brian Bahr/Getty

Title page: *Teamwork and enthusiasm are principal elements of successful cheerleading squads at every level, from junior high school to college.*

Editor: Frank Sloan

Library of Congress Cataloging-in-Publication Data

Hughes, Morgan, 1957-
  Cheerleading / Morgan Hughes.
     p. cm. -- (Junior sports)
  Includes bibliographical references and index.
  ISBN 1-59515-194-X (hardcover)
  1. Cheerleading--Juvenile literature. I. Title. II. Series: Hughes, Morgan, 1957- Junior sports.
  LB3635.H84 2004
  791.6'4--dc22
                                        2004009374

Printed in the USA

CG/CG

TABLE OF CONTENTS

IS IT A SPORT?

The first question many people ask is if cheerleading is a sport or an activity that supports other sporting events? Cheerleading has changed a lot over the years. Today it's known for its athleticism, entertainment, and even student leadership. Both physical and mental skills are developed through cheerleading.

The sport of cheerleading is an excellent way to build teamwork skills.

Ask any cheerleader and he or she will tell you: it's a sport! The skill involved, the hours of training, and the high level of competition all add up to a demanding discipline that is much more than just an after-school activity.

You have to be in good shape to perform many of the jumps in a cheerleading routine.

THE EARLY DAYS

Cheerleading dates back to 1870, with a men's glee club at Princeton University. In the 1920s, women at the University of Minnesota added tumbling **routines**. Later, the former Baltimore Colts of the National Football League created the first pro cheerleading squad.

Since the 1970s, Pop Warner has recognized cheerleading and conducted many successful programs for young athletes in this fast-growing activity.

SAFETY FIRST

Every cheerleading coach needs to create an environment where safety is the highest priority. In addition to its cheers and dance routines, cheerleading includes some potentially dangerous stunts that must be executed with great **precision**.

Many coaches have their teams sign a "Full-Value Contract," by which squad members agree to work together, to follow safety rules, and to practice positive teamwork.

Solid bases give Flyers confidence and help make the stunts look like fun!

To avoid injuries, each member of a cheerleading squad must be totally committed not only to his or her own safety, but also to that of every teammate. Spotters help guide and teach stunts and tricks. These spotters are experienced cheerleaders who also make sure no one is injured.

JUMPING AND DANCE

Standard cheerleading includes several jumps requiring athletic ability, strength, and flexibility. The Hurdler is a high, one-leg kick to the front. The kicking leg comes almost straight up. A whole line of cheerleaders doing the Hurdler is an inspiring sight.

The Tuck is another cheerleading jump. In this **maneuver**, both knees are brought to the chest while the arms shoot out to the sides in a V shape. A key to any good jump is snapping into position and holding the pose for as long as possible.

It is vital that any cheerleading session or practice begins with a warm-up stretch. With all the jumping and dance, pulled muscles are a constant concern.

The Tuck is a taxing jump that requires strong leg and abdominal muscles.

The Herkie is a harder jump. Like the Hurdler, it has a high, one-leg kick, but to the side instead of forward. The other leg is bent, with the knee facing the ground. Perhaps the hardest jump is the Toe Touch, with both legs lifting high and to the sides in an aerial split, with the arms pointing in a wide downward V.

The Hurdler combines agility and flexibility.

Dance is becoming a major part of cheerleading. Many teams even hire professional **choreographers** to design routines. The growing world of Hip Hop music has provided many dance steps, expanding the cultural horizon and creating new routines.

Dance routines are based on coordinated efforts by every member of the squad.

13

CHEERS AND SIDELINES

The key to effective chants is to keep them simple and to make them **rhythmic**. The chants are designed both to motivate players and to excite spectators. If they're too complicated, they won't work.

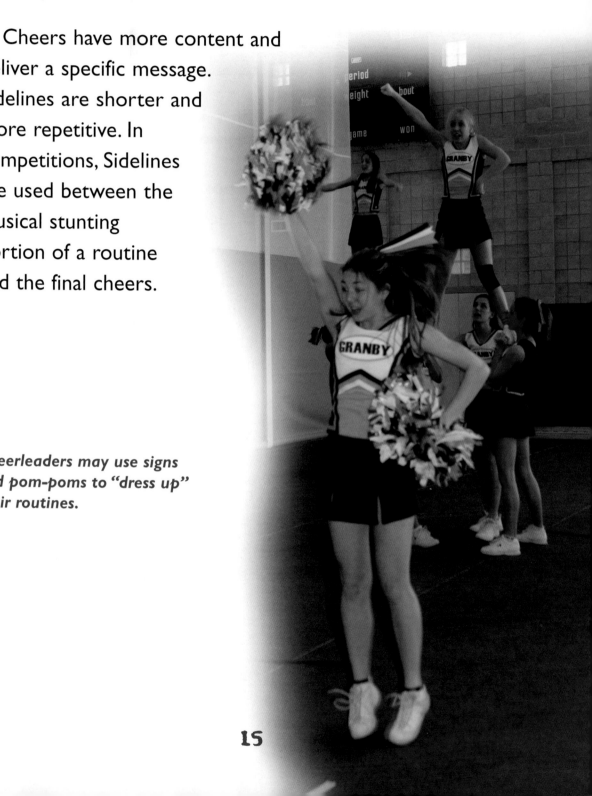

Cheers have more content and deliver a specific message. Sidelines are shorter and more repetitive. In competitions, Sidelines are used between the musical stunting portion of a routine and the final cheers.

Cheerleaders may use signs and pom-poms to "dress up" their routines.

15

HANDS AND ARMS

There are several basic hand positions. The Bucket is a palm-down fist with the thumb tucked under. The Blade has all four fingers and thumb thrust straight ahead. The Candlestick is a vertical fist with the palm facing out. The Dagger is a fist with the heel of the hand and pinky facing forward. The Knocker is a fist with the knuckles facing front.

Among the many arm positions are the T with arms out, parallel to the ground. The High V has arms held up at a slight outward angle. A Low V has arms down at a slightly outward angle. A Diagonal has one arm in a High V and the other in a Low V. An L has one arm straight up and the other straight out **parallel** to the ground.

Any arm position with bent elbows is called "broken." A Broken T is a T with the elbows bent and the fists pointing toward each other in front of the chest.

It's important to have good arm position and be in unison as a group.

Cheerleading requires precision and sharpness. Hand motions can't be sloppy, particularly the punches. The Up Punch has one fist on the hip while the other fires straight overhead. In a Punch Out or Punch Forward, both fists snap straight ahead at chest level.

The girls on the left and right show Diagonals.
The girl in the center shows a Low V.

A Cross or Front Cross is carried out when one fist shoots out to the front across the chest while the other fist stays on the hip. These positions may be used in **combination** to create different kinds of routines and different types of cheers.

Cheerleaders' props include pom-poms, banners, scarves, or ribbons. Cheerleaders may also hold up signs or decorative boxes with team **insignia**.

The young lady in the center shows a Low V with blade hands, while the young ladies on the right and left show Cross Punches.

STUNTS

Stunts are the most exciting part of cheerleading. They can be breathtaking for both the audience as well as for the participants. It's thrilling to pull off a great stunt in front of a big crowd.

The Flyers are the top part of the stunt **structure**. They are the small, athletic squad members who rely on their teammates to ensure their safety from the moment they are launched until they're back in the arms of the Catchers.

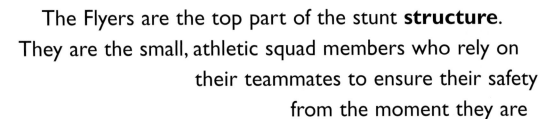

The Basket Throw shown here requires lots of practice.

The Bases are the bottom part of the stunt structure. They are the big, strong athletes who both throw and catch the Flyers. Balance and strength are critical. Spotters are very important in stunts, for they make sure Flyers don't fall through the Catchers and hit the ground.

The Thigh Stand is one of the most basic stunts for new cheerleaders. Yet it requires strength and stability in the Base and agility in the Flyers.

In the side view, notice the back member of the three-person base. Her job is to make sure the Flyer doesn't fall to the floor.

The three base members of a standard four-person stunt team share the weight of the Flyer and provide a strong support system.

TUMBLING

A key part of cheerleading is tumbling. Those who are flexible and can dance make excellent tumblers. Gymnasts can be good cheerleaders because they practice many of the same moves. Grace, artistry, speed, and strength all make up tumbling at its best.

The famous Dallas Cowboys cheerleaders are solid professionals.

A cheerleading team may build countless tumbling maneuvers into its routine. They include front and back rolls, handstands, cartwheels, round-offs, front walkovers, and back walkovers. With practice, any cheerleader can master these basics.

In addition to the basics, there are some challenging tumbles a squad may learn. These include the aerial cartwheel, the front handspring, the back handspring, the round-off back handspring, and the serial front and back handsprings.

Handsprings and flips are big parts of any cheerleading routine.

Tumbling skills include the triple combination of a round-off and back handspring into a back tuck; a back somersault in the layout position; and a "whipback" somersault. These should be taught only by an expert instructor.

Anyone training for cheerleading should consider the following: (1) power, (2) balance, (3) flexibility, and (4) body fat reduction.

COMPETITIONS

Cheerleading has become as competitive as any sport around. There are currently hundreds of organized meets and competitions all around the country. Every year, teams from large, mid-size, and small schools go head to head for school pride and recognition.

This exciting finishing stunt uses 16 members of the squad.

28

With a great deal of practice, a dedicated squad can achieve a high level of coordination.

GLOSSARY

choreographers (kor ee OG ruh furz) — people who create dance routines

combination (kom bih NAY shun) — the result of bringing together two or more elements

insignia (in SIG nee ah) — distinguishing signs

maneuver (mah NOO ver) — a physical movement requiring skill or dexterity

parallel (PAR uh lel) — being an equal distance apart at every point

precision (pree SIZH un) — showing exactness in movement or action

rhythmic (RITH mick) — happening with regularity

routines (roo TEENZ) — detailed courses of action

structure (STRUCK chur) — something made of several parts held together a particular way

Further Reading

Gruber, Beth. *Cheerleading For Fun.* Compass Point Books, 2004

Peters, Craig. *Chants, Cheers, and Jumps.* Mason Crest Publishers, 2002

Wilson, Leslie. *Ultimate Guide to Cheerleading.* Crown Publishing, 2003

Websites to Visit

American Cheerleading Federation @ www.cheeracf.com

Cheerleading.Net @ www.cheerleading.net

Cheerleading @ cheerleading.about.com

Universal Cheerleading Association @ www.varsity.com

Index

About the Author

Morgan Hughes is the author of more than 50 books on hockey, track and field, bicycling, and many other subjects. He lives in Connecticut with his wife, daughter, and son.